Balancing the Societal Dimensions of Venezuela and Colombia through the Amnesty, Reconciliation, and Reintegration (AR2) Process

A Monograph
by
MAJ Danielle J. Ngo
U.S. Army

MENS EST CLAVIS VICTORIAE

School of Advanced Military Studies
United States Army Command and General Staff College
Fort Leavenworth, Kansas

AY 2008

		Form Approved
REPORT DOCUMENTATION PAGE		*Form Approved* *OMB No. 0704-0188*

Public reporting burden for this collection of information is estimated to average 1 hour per response, including the time for reviewing instructions, searching existing data sources, gathering and maintaining the data needed, and completing and reviewing this collection of information. Send comments regarding this burden estimate or any other aspect of this collection of information, including suggestions for reducing this burden to Department of Defense, Washington Headquarters Services, Directorate for Information Operations and Reports (0704-0188), 1215 Jefferson Davis Highway, Suite 1204, Arlington, VA 22202-4302. Respondents should be aware that notwithstanding any other provision of law, no person shall be subject to any penalty for failing to comply with a collection of information if it does not display a currently valid OMB control number. **PLEASE DO NOT RETURN YOUR FORM TO THE ABOVE ADDRESS.**

1. REPORT DATE (DD-MM-YYYY) 22-05-2008	2. REPORT TYPE Monograph	3. DATES COVERED (From - To) July 2007 – May 2008
4. TITLE AND SUBTITLE Balancing the Societal Dimensions of Venezuela and Colombia through the Amnesty, Reconciliation, and Reintegration (AR2) Process		**5a. CONTRACT NUMBER**
		5b. GRANT NUMBER
		5c. PROGRAM ELEMENT NUMBER
6. AUTHOR(S) Ngo, Danielle J., Major, USA		**5d. PROJECT NUMBER**
		5e. TASK NUMBER
		5f. WORK UNIT NUMBER
7. PERFORMING ORGANIZATION NAME(S) AND ADDRESS(ES) School of Advanced Military Studies (SAMS) 250 Gibbon Avenue Fort Leavenworth, KS 66027-2134		**8. PERFORMING ORG REPORT NUMBER**
9. SPONSORING / MONITORING AGENCY NAME(S) AND ADDRESS(ES)		**10. SPONSOR/MONITOR'S ACRONYM(S)**
		11. SPONSOR/MONITOR'S REPORT NUMBER(S)

12. DISTRIBUTION / AVAILABILITY STATEMENT
Approved for Public Release; Distribution is Unlimited

13. SUPPLEMENTARY NOTES

14. ABSTRACT
See attached abstract.

15. SUBJECT TERMS
Colombia, Venezuela, amnesty, reconciliation, reintegration, conflict resolution

16. SECURITY CLASSIFICATION OF:			17. LIMITATION OF ABSTRACT	18. NUMBER OF PAGES	19a. NAME OF RESPONSIBLE PERSON Stefan J. Banach COL, U.S. Army
a. REPORT (U)	b. ABSTRACT (U)	c. THIS PAGE (U)	(U)	52	19b. PHONE NUMBER (include area code) 913-758-3302

Standard Form 298 (Rev. 8-98)
Prescribed by ANSI Std. Z39.18

ii

SCHOOL OF ADVANCED MILITARY STUDIES

MONOGRAPH APPROVAL

MAJ Danielle J. Ngo

Title of Monograph: Balancing the Societal Dimensions of Venezuela and Colombia through the Amnesty, Reconciliation, and Reintegration (AR2) Process

Approved by:

_____   Monograph Director
Michael W. Mosser, PhD

_____   Monograph Reader
Michael J. Swanson, COL, AV

_____   Director,
Stefan Banach, COL, IN   School of Advanced
                                            Military Studies

_____   Director,
Robert F. Baumann, Ph.D.   Graduate Degree
                                            Programs

Abstract

BALANCING THE SOCIETAL DIMENSIONS OF VENEZUELA AND COLOMBIA
THROUGH THE AMNESTY, RECONCILIATION, AND REINTEGRATION (AR2) PROCESS
by MAJ Danielle J. Ngo, U.S. Army, 52 pages.

This paper explains that in order for a fractured society to forge a lasting, stable peace, it requires not only a holistic approach to amnesty, reintegration, and reconciliation (AR2) but also a balance of three critical dimensions within its process: the political, security, and economic dimensions. It contends that if the process of AR2 is not complete or there is an imbalance in the system, the fractured society will either remain at an unstable peace, if contained, or move to crisis or possibly to war. On the surface, a government may seem successful in its quest at conflict resolution, but unless the problems underlying the societal fractures are balanced using the AR2 construct, stability will not endure.

This study examines the societal dimensions of the AR2 process by using a case study methodology. Through the examination of two countries, Venezuela and Colombia, it tries to understand why two countries that have common ancestries and a similar history of authoritarian governments, economic stagnation, and social injustice follow different paths towards conflict resolution. It explores how a shift in the balance of the three dimensions can change the direction and effectiveness of the AR2 process.

This author classifies both Venezuela and Colombia as societies in an unstable peace. Although Venezuela has become economically successful through the sales of its petroleum, economic wealth cannot solely stabilize a society. In order for Venezuela to secure a stable peace, it must balance its societal dimension by diversifying its economic base, continuing a politically open, democratic process, and addressing the concerns of its disenfranchised population.

The AR2 process in Colombia has been a long and violent journey that has yet to be resolved. Colombia's instability mainly stems from the continuing insurgency within its country and the narco-trafficking cartel. Because of its duration, Colombia is undergoing its second phase of its AR2 process because the first phase has yet to balance the three societal dimensions of AR2. In order for Colombia to balance those dimensions, it must continue its current security strategy but not neglect the economic dimension and the poor of its country. It must also continue the paramilitary reintegration while addressing corruption and human rights offenses.

Additionally, both systems cannot be analyzed in a vacuum. The fact that Colombia and Venezuela border one another and are economically dependent on one other has consequences to their AR2 process. It is a dynamic, complex system where a change to one dimension may affect the other dimensions in both countries in an unpredictable way.

The study concludes that although both Venezuela and Colombia have made much progress towards the stabilization of their countries, the process is not complete. The imbalance in the dimensions of the AR2 process precludes them from achieving a lasting, stable peace. They must look to balancing the societal dimensions not only within their country but realize that actions taken within their dimensions also affects the balance of the dimensions in neighboring countries.

TABLE OF CONTENTS

ILLUSTRATIONS

Introduction

Two nations in Latin America, Venezuela and Colombia, share a border and although their nations have similar traditions and culture, their state systems emerge in different and distinct configurations. In each country three interrelated dimensions of their society, the political, economic, and security, hold the key to its fractured society's success in the amnesty, reconciliation, and reintegration (AR2) process. In Venezuela, there remains a fractured political system recovering from party corruption, economic imbalance, and a coup attempt. In Colombia, the society remains fractured from decades of violence, insurgency, and narco-trafficking. By examining Venezuela and Colombia's post-conflict societies in some depth, not only might one better understand the circumstances under which such conflicts are ended, but also the institutional outcomes to which they give rise.

Venezuela and Colombia's common history of independence began in the early 1800s when a young Simón José Antonio de la Santísima Trinidad Bolívar vowed to never rest until Spanish America was free from Spanish rule.[1] In 1813, Bolívar invaded Venezuela, captured Caracas, and was proclaimed the "Libertador" by the people. Petitioning countries, such as Haiti for assistance, he continued fighting; and in 1817, after the Battle of Boyacá, he created the Angostura Congress. The Angostura Congress founded Gran Colombia, a federation of present day Colombia, Venezuela, Panama, and Ecuador. Bolívar was named president and continued to fight until South America was free of Spanish rule. From that point in South American history, rivalries, revolutions, and civil wars destroyed the unity Bolívar fought so hard to emplace. In 1830, Venezuela separated from Gran Colombia and became a sovereign country; Gran Colombia became the Republic of New Grenada and then renamed the Republic of Colombia. Their origins of independence set the stage for many commonalities between the two countries.

---

[1]Biblioteca Virtual de Simon Bolívar, "El Libertador," http://www.geocities.com/Athens/ Acropolis/7609/eng/bio.html (accessed 5 January 2008).

Besides sharing a common border, there are several similarities attributable to their shared cultures. Both countries emerged from highly repressive military dictatorships and both had to deal, at one point in their history, with insurgency, with Colombia still in the midst of it. Both countries have two of the longest standing democracies in Latin America dominated, until recently, by two main political parties; but political stability is not consolidated in either country. Distribution of wealth is uneven and due process is usually corrupt. Both countries share in common the Iberian culture, brought to Latin America from its Spanish ancestors. Some will argue that this common culture explains the tendency for these Latin American countries to lean towards authoritarianism, centralization, hierarchy, and militarism. In addition, the economies of Venezuela and Colombia possess features that distort the "free market" model because both states have been extensively involved in public and private enterprises, and oil in Venezuela and drugs in Colombia further distort the picture.[2] Thus, while both countries have similar characteristics, today, the differences are more emphasized and evident.

In order to understand how the AR2 construct relates to Venezuela and Colombia, one must first understand what AR2 is. In theory, AR2 is a comprehensive approach to conflict resolution in which the concepts of amnesty, reconciliation, and reintegration are used to repair a fractured society. Amnesty is a type of forgiveness or impunity and in this context, political in nature. In some cases, granting rebel leaders of groups this provisional and limited immunity has facilitated the reconciliation process. Reconciliation in itself is usually a long, broad process involving a change in the attitudes, feelings, and even beliefs between those who suffered and those who inflicted the suffering. It is part of a healing process that is necessary for long-term peace. Reintegration is the social and economic reinsertion and inclusion of the disenfranchised population back into civilian life. Ideally, the offenders should be reintegrated within the society

---

[2]Lawrence E. Harrison, *Latin America: Democracy and the Market are Not Enough* (Farmington Hills, MI: Heldref Publications, 1993), http://www.highbeam.com/doc/1G1-14625629.html (accessed 16 March 2008).

because their continued exclusion from the community could reinvigorate the instability already present.[3] These AR2 concepts are viewed as a cohesive way to restore a post-conflict society, and in Venezuela and Colombia, the divergent application of these concepts is what differentiates the direction the countries are headed today.

The AR2 process in Colombia today is proceeding in fits and starts amidst a long history of war and violence. The main hurdles are the reintegration of the guerilla and paramilitary groups and the suppression of the illicit drug trade. Although there is some progress within President Álvaro Uribe's administration, there is still much work needed to complete the process.

The AR2 process is much further along in Venezuela although the period of democracy spans a shorter period, Venezuela underwent a series of dictatorships before democracy was finally implemented in 1958 and even then, the democracy was characterized by political unrest, assassination attempts and coups. Instability still remains, as the AR2 process is not yet complete.

President Hugo Chávez's policies favor a populist movement which has led to an ideological difference of both governments today with Colombia as pro-American and Venezuela as anti-American. In addition, Venezuela has increased social spending for the poor and promotes a restrictive economic policy. Colombia, on the other hand, is a strong supporter of Washington's free trade policies. Recently, differences in those countries have led to escalated tensions caused from the Columbian government's killing of the second in command of the purportedly Venezuela-sponsored narco-terrorist group Revolutionary Armed Forces of Columbia (FARC).

How can two countries that have come from the same path, with a history of authoritarian governments, economic stagnation, and social injustice, seem to be heading in different directions today? Does each country's implementation of the AR2 process have something to do with this divergence?

_____

[3]International Institute for Democracy and Electoral Assistance (IDEA). *Reconciliation After Conflict: Policy Summary* (Sweden: Bulls Tryckeri, 2003), 10. www.idea.int/publications/reconciliation/upload/policy_summary.pdf (accessed 15 March 2008).

Case Selection and Methodology

This monograph describes the history and conditions in which both Venezuela and Colombia have arrived at their individual stages in the AR2 process. It then attempts to assess the dynamic interrelationship dimensions of Dr. Michael Mosser's amnesty, reconciliation, and reintegration (AR2) model using the empirical case studies of Venezuela and Colombia. This dimensional model suggests that in order to effectively reconstruct a fractured society, all three dimensions; the political, security, and economic, must be completely integrated and balanced.[4] This model is depicted in figure 1:

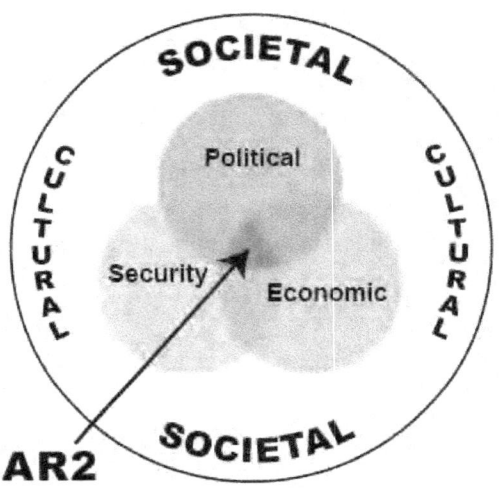

Figure 1.   Dimensions of the AR2 Process
Source: Michael W. Mosser, "The 'Armed Reconciler:' The Military Role in Amnesty, Reconciliation, and Reintegration Process," *Military Review* 87, no. 6 (November-December 2007): 14.

Dr. Mosser's AR2 model is relevant to both countries because both Venezuela and Colombia are societies that are considered fractured today in that throughout their history, they have undergone cycles of turmoil that have not ended in a lasting peace. The three dimensions;

---

[4]Dr. Michael W. Mosser, "The 'Armed Reconciler:' The Military Role in Amnesty, Reconciliation, and Reintegration Process," *Military Review* 87, no. 6 (November-December 2007): 13.

the political, security, and economic, are not balanced within both the countries' socio-cultural framework. This author considers both Venezuela and Colombia as "unstable peace" countries based upon Michael Lund's "Life Cycle of International Conflict" diagram (see figure 2). In his book *Preventing Violent Conflicts*, Lund presents this diagram where different measures are proposed depending on the intensity of violence and the progression of deteriorations in a conflict relationship.[5]

The line that forms an arc from left to right across the diagram portrays the course of a conflict as it rises and falls in intensity over time. Of significance is the concept that each conflict that has abated can re-escalate. This is the case in Venezuela and Colombia's history where conflict has ebbed and flowed many times. In Lund's diagram, this author would argue that Colombia's present location is on the left side of the arch in "unstable peace" while Venezuela is on the right side of the arch in "unstable peace". This author contends that they both are unstable because the political, economic, and security dimensions are not balanced. The importance is for both countries to implement post-conflict peace building to obtain a durable peace and prevent the arch from rising again. In order to do this, there must be a balance using the dimensional model.

---

[5]State, Society and Governance in Malenesia Project, "Conflict and Post-conflict: Asia Pacific Dimensions" (Workshop, University House, Australian national University, 23-24 September 2002), 24. http://rspas.anu.edu.au/papers/melanesia/conference_papers/2002/ 0209_conflict_Report.pdf (accessed 18 February 2008).

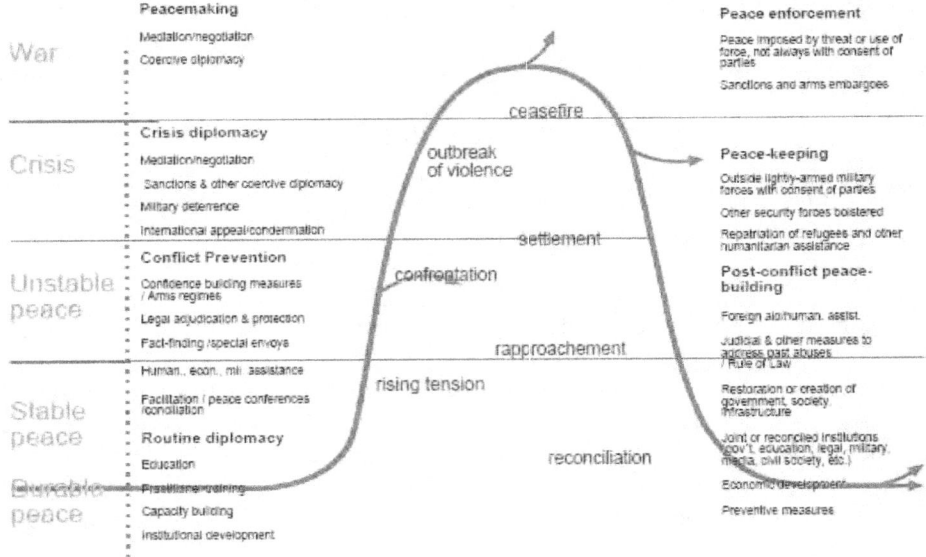

Figure 2.   Life Cycle of Int'l Conflict Management
Source: State, Society and Governance in Malenesia Project, "Conflict and Post-conflict: Asia Pacific Dimensions," (Workshop, University House, Australian national University, 23-24 September 2002), 24.

In order to apply the AR2 model, both countries must be considered at some stage of post-conflict. Both of these countries are in the post-conflict phase because, as Dr. Norbert Ropers describes, some of the characteristics that describe post-conflict management include peace-keeping, political reconstruction and the creation of new "inclusive" political structures, physical reconstruction, and the "civilization" of society by working through and coming to terms with the past.[6] To varying degrees, each country has integrated these post-conflict management techniques.

---

[6]Dr. Norbert Ropers, *Peace-Building, Crisis Prevention and Conflict Management: Technical Cooperation in the Context of Crises, Conflicts and Disasters* (Federal Republic of Germany: Deutsche Gesellschaft für, 2002), 37. www.gtz.de/de/dokumente/en-crisis-prevention-and-conflict-management.pdf (accessed 18 February 2008).

Amnesty, reconciliation, and reintegration via a holistic approach in which all three of these elements are present in each of these case studies will be examined. The question is not, therefore, if they exist but how the political, economic, and security dimensions have affected the ability for AR2 to be successful. As one shifts from Dr. Mosser's AR2 theory to practice, this author will examine how the three dimensions have evolved from their roots of conflict in each country. Venezuela and Colombia are chosen here to not only provide examples of the dimensions within the AR2 framework but also contrast how the shift in balance of the three dimensions can change the direction and effectiveness of the AR2 process. Then the imbalance in each country and what is needed to shift the dimensions into equilibrium will be assessed. In comparison, this author will depict how two countries, sharing a border, with the same historical traditions and culture, can end up with an AR2 process that is seemingly headed in different directions and yet ironically pulls each country together. Finally, this author will address how one can learn from the imbalance of the societal dimensions within the AR2 model in Venezuela and Colombia and the broad consequences thereof for United States policy.

VENEZUELA

Roots of Conflict: The Need for AR2

In order to examine the AR2 process in Venezuela, one must briefly delve into the history and the roots of conflict within the country. From 1830 when Venezuela separated from Gran Colombia until the emergence of pro-democratic movements in 1958, the country had practically continuous dictatorial rule. Ruled for most of the first half of the twentieth century by a succession of military dictators, pro-democratic groups forced the military out of politics in 1958, and implemented a new constitution in 1961. Since that time, Venezuela has had uninterrupted civilian constitutional rule.[7]

Feeding off oil revenues as its fundamental source of wealth, Venezuela shifted from an agricultural and rural-based society to an industrial and urban-based society. Before the oil era began in the mid-1920s, about 70 percent of the Venezuelan population was rural, illiterate, and poor. Over the next fifty years, the ratios were reversed so that over 88 percent of the population became urban and literate.[8] Economic success and expansion brought about high rates of growth, low inflation, and balanced external accounts giving the populist-minded political and government elites excuses to put off carrying out significant economic reforms.[9] Instead, during times of economic booms, the government, interest groups, politicians, and bureaucrats increased their hold on the oil industry to increase their share of power. This led to government inefficiency and corruption and when there was a shock to the system, it crippled the Venezuelan economy because of a lack of economic diversity. Poor economic policies and a collapse of oil prices in the 1980s resulted in increased poverty, crime, and public dissatisfaction.

In February 1992, Lieutenant Colonel Hugo Chávez Frias led a group of military officers on an unsuccessful coup attempt on President Carlos Andrés Pérez citing the 1989 Caracazo riots as evidence of popular unrest. Chávez was imprisoned, and a year later Congress impeached Pérez for corruption. Chávez was released from prison in 1994 and attained folk-hero status while there. Up to that point, the president had always been a representative of one of the two traditional parties, the Democratic Action Party (AD) or the Social Christian Party (COPEI).

---

[7]Library of Congress, Federal Research Division, "Country Profile: Venezuela," (March 2005): 3. http://lcweb2.loc.gov/frd/cs/profiles/Venezuela.pdf (accessed 20 December 2007).

[8]Richard A. Haggerty, ed., *Venezuela: A Country Study* (Washington, DC: Government Printing Office for the Library of Congress, 1990), http://countrystudies.us/venezuela/13.htm (accessed on 15 December 2008)

[9]Manuel Hidalgo, "A Petro-State: Oil, Politics and Democracy in Venezuela" (Working Paper 49/007, 11 June 2007), 4. www realinstitutoelcano.org/documentos/WP2007/WP49-2007_Hidalgo_Petro-State_Venezuela.pdf (accessed 8 March 2008).

Frequent economic crises and prevalent corruption eventually led to a collapse in their support and a call for radical political reform. Taking advantage of the population's desire for new leadership and disillusionment of the corrupt and inept institutions, Hugo Chávez won the presidential election in 1998 with an overwhelming majority.

Chávez took strong control of Venezuelan politics through a series of elections, referenda, and decrees. His supporters believed this was necessary to get rid of an old, corrupt order and build a more just society. His critics believed it showed his authoritarian tendencies and intention to keep a firm grip on power. Chávez's opposition included businessmen, much of the middle class, senior military officers, and parts of organized labor. They believed Chávez was leading the country to economic ruin and a leftist dictatorship.

In April 2002, significant economic decline helped lead to a general strike and a demand for Chávez's resignation. After violence broke out, senior military officers overthrew Chávez and installed business leader Pedro Carmona Estanga as the interim president. Chávez supporters took to the streets protesting his removal from office, and with the support of a group of loyal generals, they were able to have Chávez reinstated only two days after his overthrow. In the wake of the aborted coup, Venezuela grew even more fractured with Chávez's popularity decreasing from 80 percent to 30 percent and with almost all of his support from the poor.[10]

At the end of 2002, opponents called another prolonged strike, but under substantial international pressure, they turned their efforts instead to the political process and implemented a recall vote to remove Chávez from office. International mediation was required to settle the dispute. When the referendum was finally held in August 2004, Chávez received the support of 59 percent of those voting in fair and free elections. In October, Chávez and his coalition won another sweeping victory at local and state elections. Then, in the 2005 National Assembly

---

[10]Alex Bellos, "Chávez Rises From Very Peculiar Coup," *The Guardian* (15 April 2002), http://www.guardian.co.uk/world/2002/apr/15/venezuela.alexbellos (accessed 18 May 2008).

elections, Chávez's party and allied parties won all 167 seats after the increasingly incompetent opposition dropped out.[11]

Chávez's radical policy program has exacerbated political polarization, but he has survived several attempts to remove him from power. Overall, Chávez has been politically victorious. However, in December 2007, Chávez lost a referendum on constitutional reform, bolstering a newly emerging opposition movement centered on students and disenchanted "chavistas," or Chávez supporters.

In January 2008, Chávez granted amnesty to select members of the opposition groups of the 2002 coup and the oil strike. He did not grant amnesty to "those persons who have committed crimes against humanity, grave violations of human rights, and crimes of war," or "those who are fugitives from justice, those who never wanted to recognize Venezuelan institutions."[12] Critics of the amnesty decree say that those charged with the coup are victims of political persecution. Others, like the hierarchy of the Catholic Church in Venezuela believe some of the crimes and charges are spurious or "confusing" and that the amnesty should be broadened.

The current problems in Venezuela are the remaining tensions after the attempted coup on Chávez and the reasons that underpin it to include political polarization and the disenfranchisement of the middle and upper class. Although Chávez has just granted amnesty to some of the members of his opposition, criticism still exists on the scope of that decree. In addition, the reintegration of the opposition back into political arena is not complete and reconciliation with the middle and elite groups is tentative and unsteady.

---

[11]Christopher L. Brown and Alyssa Smith, Latin America in Transition: Lesson 2, Politics and Democracy (Southern Center for International Studies, 2007), 1-2. www.southerncenter.org/ la_jan07_lesson2.pdf (accessed 2 April 2008).

[12]Kiraz Janicke, "Venezuela President's Amnesty for Coup Participants is Praised and Criticised," 3 January 2008, http://www.venezuelanalysis.com/news/3030 (accessed 15 May 2008).

The AR2 process in Venezuela, although on the downward slope of Lund's conflict cycle, is not yet completed nor is its society dimensions balanced. It has the potential to cycle back to increasing levels of intensity if the current dimensional imbalances are not corrected.

AR2 in Practice (in Venezuela)

The societal dimensions of AR2 in Venezuela, as it is with Colombia, are not balanced. Although Venezuela is on the downward slope of Lund's cycle, it does not imply that it would take longer than Colombia to cycle back to crisis. An adjustment to Lund's diagram below (see figure 3) depicts that it is feasible that although Venezuela appears more stable than Colombia today, Venezuela may elevate to crisis and war-level in a shorter time span given the imbalance of conditions in the three AR2 dimensions.

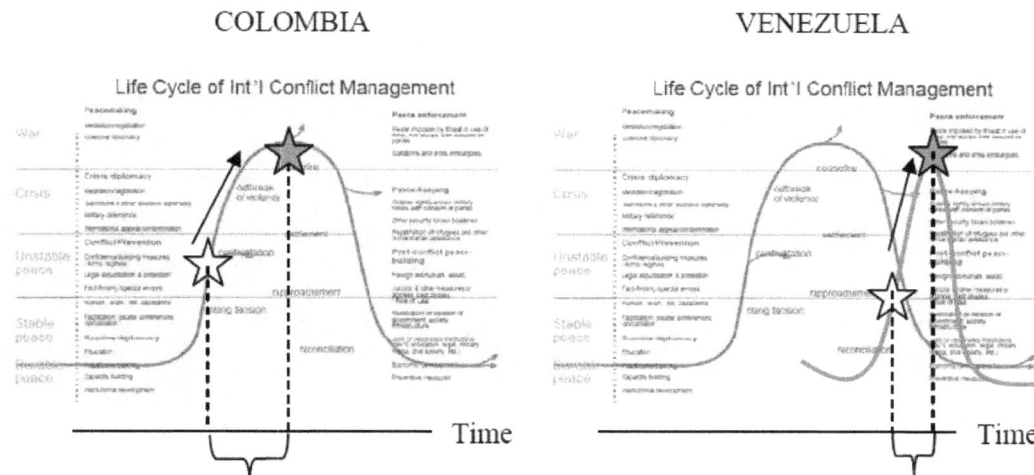

Figure 3.   Possible Time Compaction Via Rise in Conflict
Source: State, Society and Governance in Malenesia Project, "Conflict and Post-conflict: Asia Pacific Dimensions" (Workshop, University House, Australian national University, 23-24 September 2002), 24.

This is significant because if the three dimensions of Venezuela's AR2 process are not managed correctly, the consequence may be a sharp rise back into conflict. The three dimensions of the AR2 model are depicted below (see figure 4) for Venezuela in which the economic dimension overwhelms the other two dimensions.

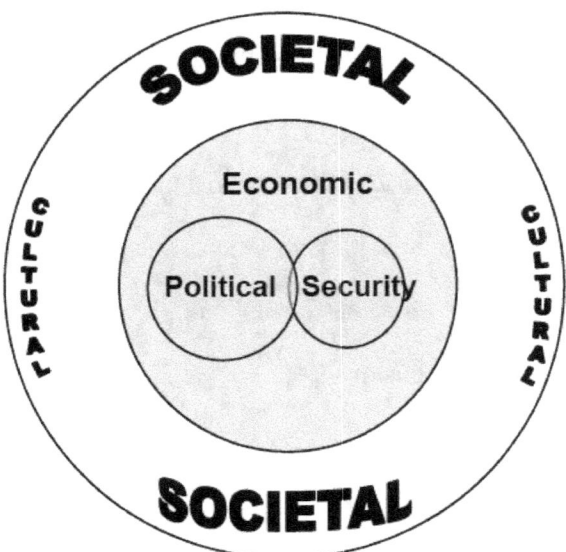

Figure 4.   Venezuela's Societal Dimensions of AR2

In Venezuela's socio-cultural framework, the imbalance stems from the fact that the economic dimension dominates Venezuela's AR2 process. The economic dimension, through exploitation of petroleum, has become fundamental to the country's socio-economic and political modernization; so much so in fact that everything seems to hinge on that one product.

The ideal case of balance would be one in which each dimension within the society is present in abundance but does not overwhelm the others. Also, the society should popularly accept and be receptive to the dimensional structure. This author would argue that Venezuela AR2 has the systems in place to balance the three dimensions, but retains enough instability to force another cycle of conflict.

Imbalanced AR2 Societal Dimensions

All three dimensions in Venezuela are currently imbalanced today. President Chávez has the political and security dimensions of AR2 much more balanced at the moment than the economic dimension. Both the political and security dimensions continue to need balancing but much more emphasis is needed to balance the economic dimension. If all three dimensions are balanced, Venezuela has a great potential to achieve sustainable economic and social development.

Political Dimension

In the political dimension, President Chávez has had much success and yet this dimension continues to remain unbalanced. His success stems from his popular election to the presidency in 1999 with a new constitution providing possibly reelection to an additional six-year consecutive term. Chávez's policies, synonymous with populism, gained him increasing popular support as he instituted social programs for the poor, challenged traditional elites, and asserted national autonomy in the international arena. Furthermore, in the political dimension, the Venezuelan government has a balance of power through it structure of the executive, legislative, and judicial branches in addition to two new powers, Citizen Power and the Electoral Power. The two new powers further distribute governmental power to the people. The Citizen Power is comprised of officials who are responsible for overseeing, investigating, and punishing administrative irregularities and defending civil virtues and democratic principles. The Electoral Power is responsible for organizing elections at all levels. An example of this balance of power was when Chávez called for changes to the constitution in August 2007 to end presidential term limits, limit central bank autonomy, strengthen state expropriation powers, and provide for public control over international reserves. Although the National Assembly approved the changes, the public defeated this referendum in December 2007 with a 51 percent rejection vote.[13] The balance of the political dimension of AR2 allows Chávez to use his political power to deliver on some of his social spending promises to his lower-class supporters. Although he lost the referendum, he was only defeated by a small margin. Because of this, many are concerned about his efforts to increase state control over the economy, put military personnel into key political and economic positions, quiet dissent, and associate Venezuela with rogue regimes around the world. His policies are likely to lead to additional tensions, as politicians wrangle for position. Here, the political balance is offset because of the fear that the Venezuela has the potential to shift from a democratic state to authoritarian or totalitarian control under Chávez. If that political dimension shifts further away from a balance of power, this will cause an increase in instability.

Other potential problems to maintaining a balance in the political dimension include Chávez's 2004 legislation to increase the Supreme Court, or Tribuna Suprema de Justicia (TSJ) from 20 to 32 justices. Critics such as Human Rights Watch stated that this law amounted to a "political takeover" of the court thereby giving Chávez near-absolute control of the courts.[14] Chávez's increased power and control are worrisome for those who fear Chávez's potential for running an authoritarian regime. Enhancing those worries is the fact that President Chávez is the commander in chief of a reorganized armed force called the National Armed Force (FAN- Fuerza Armada Nacional). The National Defense Council advises the president on national security matters and the Higher Council of the Armed Forces advises him on defense matters. Although Venezuela has had a long history of civilian rule, the FAN has become a politicized force under a military defense minister who purges the force of any members disloyal to Chávez. Although the

[13]Daniel Cancel and Sara Miller Llana, "Hugo Chávez Suffers a Blow to His 'Revolution,'" *Christian Science Monitor*, 4 December 2007, http://www.csmonitor.com/2007/1204/p01s01-woam html (accessed 19 May 2008).

[14]Kevin Sullivan, "Chávez Tightening Grip on Judges, Critics Charge Venezuelan President's Reforms Called Threat to Rule of Law, Attempt to Undermine Recall Effort," *Washington Post Foreign Service*, (20 June 2004): A24, http://www.washingtonpost.com/wp-dyn/articles/A54913-2004Jun19.html (accessed 18 March 2008)

previous constitution stated that the military was expected to be "apolitical, obedient, and non-deliberating," the 1999 constitution states only that the military should be "without militancy."[15] The new constitution also gives the president the authority to make military promotions without legislative approval and allows the military the right to vote. The worry is that the increased military will be used to support Chávez's political, possibly anti-democratic, endeavors and that Chávez's presidentialism can be perverted into quasi-authoritarianism or even dictatorship.

Another fear of semi-authoritarianism is the absorption of the political parties that support Chávez's policies. In December 2006, in the wake of his third presidential victory, Chávez announced his intention to unite these various elements into a single party, the Partido Socialista Unido de Venezuela (PSUV), a left wing political party founded in order to merge all 24 parties that supported the "Bolívarian Revolution", Chávez's movement to reshape the economic and political structures in Venezuela. According to Chávez, he wanted to unite all his supporters in order to prevent sectarianism, infighting, and corruption.[16] Critics claim that this is another method for Chávez to gain absolute control. These issues could compound the other problems in the political dimension, and further shift this dimension away from the balance needed for a successful AR2 process. Therefore, most observers agree that the biggest obstacle to stable growth in Venezuela today is the country's polarized political climate.

Security Dimension

The security dimension is fairly balanced at the moment with internal threats to Venezuela limited to acts of crime. However, if the security forces do not keep the violence in check, the security dimension may tilt out of balance and that potential for an increased security

---

[15]Library of Congress, 25.

[16]Sujatha Fernandes, "Political Parties and Social Change in Venezuela," *Venezuela News, Views, and Analysis*, Venezuelanalysis.com, 22 March 2007, http://www.venezuelanalysis.com/analysis/2295 (accessed 14 May 2008).

threat lurks. Violent crime is a major problem in the bigger cities, in particular Caracas, which has one of the highest crime rates in South America. Venezuela's homicide rate has more than doubled since the early 1990s with 11,900 murders reported in 2003, as compared with only 2,000 in 1991.[17]

Although Chávez rarely publicly discusses the country's soaring crime rates and official statistics on crime are closely guarded, the Venezuelan capital has become extremely violent. Recent estimates of its homicide rate would place Caracas among the most dangerous cities in the world. Since the Venezuelan government stopped releasing official homicide rates in 2003 after the number of killings reached nearly 12,000 countrywide that year, these estimates are tentative. Unofficial estimates for 2006 put the number of homicides in Caracas alone at 6,000. That is more than 100 slayings per 100,000 inhabitants.[18] By comparison, in 2006 the highest homicide rate in the United States was in Detroit where there were 23.7 slayings per 100,000 inhabitants.[19]

The homicide rate is just one of Venezuela's security problems. Since the government curtailed its cooperation with foreign governments on counter narcotics, South American drug traffickers face less police scrutiny in Venezuela than they do in other countries. Venezuela, for example, suspended its cooperation with the U.S. Drug Enforcement Administration (DEA) in 2005 after Caracas accused the agency of spying on behalf of the United States.[20] International cooperation is crucial in dealing with issues, such as drug trafficking, given that illegal shipments

---

[17]Monte Reel, "Crime Brings Venezuelans Into Streets: Large Protests Over Soaring Homicide Rate Create Political Challenge for Chávez," *Washington Post*, 10 May 2006: A17.

[18]Globalsecurity.org, "Venezuela- Military," http://www.globalsecurity.org/military/world/ venezuela/intro htm (accessed 19 May 2008).

[19]U.S. Department of Justice, Federal Bureau of Investigation, "2007 Preliminary Semiannual Uniform Crime Report- Table 4: Offenses Reported to Law Enforcement, by State by City 100,000 and over in Population," 7 January 2008, http://www fbi.gov/ucr/prelim2007/index html (accessed 19 May 2008).

[20]Embassy of the Bolivarian Republic of Venezuela in the United States of America, "Venezuela's War on Drug Trafficking," http://www.embavenez-us.org/news.php?nid=4182 (accessed 14 February 2008).

pass through multiple borders on their way from production to market. How can Venezuela balance the security dimension if they dispose of the tools that have assisted them without replacing that capability through other sources?

Compounding the problems is the country's endemic corruption, which extends from police on the street to the courts. In an October interview, Venezuelan Attorney General Isaías Rodríguez tried to belie claims that the country's judicial system is incapable of effectively dealing with drug traffickers but freely admitted that "we have received information that some police officials from the judicial police and some officials of the armed forces have extended authorizations and have given protection to some narco-traffickers. For us, it's in the process of investigation."[21]

Security is not much better outside the capital, especially along Venezuela's extensive land border with Colombia, where guerrilla groups have been known to move freely between the two countries. Official corruption is a particular problem in this area as well, considering that one of the most notorious Venezuelan groups linked to Colombian guerrillas--the Cartel of the Suns-- allegedly is run by Venezuelan National Guard generals. According to DEA estimates, the group moves up to 5 tons of illegal drugs per month from Colombia into Venezuela.[22] Venezuela has long been used as a transshipment hub for narcotics smuggling and as a gateway in the Americas for illegal aliens attempting to reach the United States from Asia and the Middle East. Venezuela cannot guarantee stability when the livelihood of its people increasingly depends on illegal drugs.

In addition to drug trafficking, organized crime groups in Venezuela have found kidnapping to be an increasingly lucrative business. According to the U.S. Embassy in Caracas, more than 1,000 kidnappings were reported from 2006 to 2007 and at least 45 foreigners were

---

[21]Juan Forero, "Interview with Venezuela's Attorney General," *Washington Post*, 26 October 2007, http://www.washingtonpost.com/wp-dyn/content/article/2007/10/25/AR2007102501465.html (accessed 18 May 2008).

[22]The group's name comes from the insignia worn on the officers' uniforms.

kidnapped during the first eight months of 2007.[23] There also is a political aspect to kidnapping cases, as the wealthy victims are often viewed as capitalists, people considered at odds with the goals and ideals of Chávez's Bolivarian Revolution. Because of this, victims and their families often do not receive sympathetic treatment from the authorities when such crimes are reported. One of the necessities of a successful AR2 process is to provide the people within the society a safe and secure environment. If the people do not feel safe within that country, the eventual paralysis will eviscerate the balance of the security dimension.

So far, the Chávez government's efforts to counter the trends of violence throughout the country have been minimal. In the case of high-profile killings, authorities reportedly round up suspects quickly, but rarely produce evidence linking any of the detainees to the crime. Only a small percentage of criminals are ever tried and convicted. Moreover, violent crimes frequently occur during daylight hours and even in public areas such as Caracas' Maiquetía Airport and in popular tourist attractions, such as the Avila National Park.

Further complicating matters are reports that security forces and parts of the judicial system have become increasingly politicized as a result of the government's practice of keeping and promoting officials for their loyalty to Chávez's Bolivarian ideals rather than their interest in, or their ability to fight, crime. These politicized officials also have hesitated to root out police corruption or crack down on criminals in poor areas because such areas are bastions of Chávez supporters. Additionally, the recent crackdowns on student protesters suggest the government is heavily focused on using security forces to quell its opposition rather than to fight crime. In July 2007, Chávez chided student groups protesting constitutional reforms aimed at consolidating his power, calling the students patsies of the United States. On 1 November 2007, police dispersed student demonstrators with tear gas and water cannons. From 2005 to 2006, the government

---

[23]Stratfor, Strategic Forecasting, Inc., "Venezuela: Security Takes a Backseat," 2 November 2007, http://www.stratfor.com/analysis/venezuela_security_takes_backseat (accessed 18 February 2008).

suppressed 74 demonstrations violations with at least 71 injuries by bullets, blows, choking, and other mistreatment.[24] The government's weak response to date and its focus on suppressing any opposition suggest the security environment in Venezuela will continue to deteriorate. Besides this internal security situation, Venezuela must also deal with external security issues.

Compounding the internal security problems are the external security issues that include the narco-terrorism crossing state borders and territorial disputes with Colombia and Guyana. If the security environment deteriorates, the AR2 process will destabilize further.

Economic Dimension

The economic dimension, which is the least balanced, relies on oil revenues as Venezuela's primary source of wealth and thus the term "rentismo" is used to describe this practice where the government uses a single resource as the pillar of the economy and its main tool to manage the country.[25] In the past, the "rentismo" structure actually hurt countries because it did not develop a competitive, diverse economic base. It relied predominantly on one source thereby overlooking long-term growth and stability.

The greatest growth to Venezuela's economic situation is its vast oil reserves and the revenues generated from it sales. When Hugo Chávez came into power in 1999, oil was less than US$10 per barrel, and today the recent high is over US$130 per barrel. Previously, the oil industry transferred from an autonomous institution to a State-run company where Chávez now uses this dimension in great overlap with the political dimension. This socio-political model is supposed to enhance the so-called new Socialism of the 21st century in which the Venezuelan

---

[24]Rafael Uzcátegui, "Venezuela 2006: Continued Repression of Popular Protest," *El Libertario*, March 2007, www nodo50.org/ellibertario/english/repressionofpopularprotest.doc (accessed 14 May 2008).

[25]Hidalgo, 1.

government uses the oil to create anti-capitalist or anti-U.S. coalitions. Unfortunately, the model he is using is limiting and is questionable for long-term development.

So why does the economic dimension seem to be working in the AR2 construct of Venezuela under Chávez, or does it? Since Chávez took power, the government has had greater visibility and impact because of the growing oil revenues. Using these oil revenues, Chávez has launched a series of social measures seeking to improve the living conditions for broad sectors of the population. His increased popularity with the people has broadened his power over time and has given him the ability to control all of the State's power and almost all of the representative bodies. Chávez now reigns over the so-called *Bolivarian Revolution* referring to the building of a new kind of socialism to improve the living conditions of the poor.[26] His appeal to the masses continues to increase as well as his power base.

To build upon the old concept of "rentismo" which had its limitations, Chávez has implemented new economic policies including creating pacts with fellow OPEC members to raise prices and cut production. Also, to guarantee more stable tax revenues, he instituted the Gaseous Hydocarbons Law (1999), the Liquid Hydocarbons Law (2001), and reforms of the Income Tax Law in which the State Ministry administers licenses for hydrocarbon exploitation instead of the oil industry, 20 to 30 percent royalties are imposed for hydrocarbon, and the State holds majority stake for the more profitable upstream hydrocarbon activities.[27] Upstream activities are the processes of extracting the oil and refining it while downstream is the commercial side of the business such as delivering heating oil or gas stations. To further boost tax revenue, Chávez has taken steps to re-nationalize the oil industry by creating new taxes and raising royalty rates and income tax on foreign investment.

_____

[26]Ibid., 9.

[27]Ibid, 10.

Economic success during Chávez's tenure is evident in the statistics. Since Chávez's 1999 presidency, the household poverty rate has reduced by 11.4 percent (2005) and the individual poverty rate has been reduced by 12.6 percent (2005).[28] The unemployment rate dropped from 14.9 percent in 1999 to an eight-year low of 8.4 percent in 2006.[29] The Gross Domestic Product, although it fell by 1 percent to 2 percent from 1999 to 2003, has notably increased to 17.8 percent in 2004 and 9 percent in 2005.[30] Since 2003, Chávez has implemented a series of programs called social "missions" that have raised the revenue for the poor, provided health care, subsidized food, and increased educational access. Overall social spending has increased steadily from 8.2 percent GDP in 1998 to 12.5 percent in 2006.[31] On the surface, Venezuela seems to have success in this dimension of AR2. However, it is speculative how well this will work in the mid to long term.

There are perhaps indicators now that suggest that unless Chávez revamps his fiscal policy, there may be serious problems ahead for the economy, thus putting the balance of the economic dimension in a downward spiral. Potential problems include a decline in oil production as a result of the new taxes and increased royalty rates. Private investors are less willing to become part of a joint venture because their profit margins are decreasing under these new regulations. The oil sector, the primary economic stimulator in Venezuela, is highly dependent on external variables and is limited by production capacity. This makes Venezuela highly susceptible to times of market decline. Furthermore, with the increase in oil revenues came the expansion of the administration, State-run companies, and government agencies. This increase in the

---

[28]Mark Weisbrot, Luis Sandoval, and David Rosnick, (CEPR), *Poverty Rates in Venezuela: Getting the Numbers Right* (Washington, DC: Center for Economic and Policy Research, May 2006), 3. www.cepr net/documents/venezuelan_poverty_rates_2006_05.pdf (accessed 9 March 2008).

[29]Theresa Bradley, and Guillermo Parra-Bernal, "Venezuela's Unemployment Rate Falls to 8.4 Percent (Update 1)" *Bloomberg.com* (25 January 2007), www.bloomberg.com/apps/news?pid=20601086&sid=aCwKpgiCRX10&refer=news (accessed 18 February 2008).

[30]Hidalgo, 13.

[31]Weisbrot et al., 6.

administration has led to an increase in State capitalism and in turn has led to inefficiency, waste, and loss of productivity. The government continues to nationalize more industries like the telephone company, CANTV and media outlets like local radio and television stations, leading some analysts to describe Venezuela as a "predator State," whereas the State appropriates what other sectors of society produce instead of producing its own wealth.[32]

Inflation, which has been high since 2002 when the Bolívar was floated, declined through 2005 and in 2006 soared to 17 percent, which was the highest in any Latin American country, and at the end of the year in 2007 reached 22.5 percent.[33] Investors, wary of the government's interventionist economic policies, also have been dumping the local currency. Also contributing to inflation are years of rising oil export revenues, the government's stimulatory fiscal spending, and fast-growing domestic demand. In addition, the government remains reluctant to cut back significantly on its spending.

The economic structure does not seem to be in place for long-term sustainability. Venezuela has become "a collector and distributor of income rather than an engine for development."[34] If the State cannot handle its influx of revenue, Chávez's fiscal policies may exacerbate more now, than in the past, and be unable to recover from any significant economic downturn.

The economic dimension seems to be the pivotal point in the dimensional model in this case. With oil as Venezuela's main economic resource and with the government nationalizing industries like steel and media, the economic dimension seems to encompass all of Venezuelan society. Oil revenue is also being used as Chávez's major tool in the AR2 process. This alone cannot balance the economic dimension let alone balance all three dimensions. According to

---

[32]Ibid., 12.

[33]"Venezuela's New Bolívar," The Economist Intelligence Unit ViewsWire, 3 January 2008, http://www.economist.com/displaystory.cfm?story_id=10436099 (accessed 19 February 2008).

[34]Hidalgo, 15.

Misagh Parsa in his book, *States, Ideologies, & Social Revolutions*, declining economic opportunities establish the conditions for revolution. There is a danger here because the economic dimension seems to disproportionately dominate the other two political and security dimensions instead of a balance of all three within the AR2 process. It seems that without the power the economic dimension bears, the political and security dimensions would collapse as it has several times in Venezuela's past.

How to Make it Work

In terms of balancing the dimensions of society via an AR2 process, it seems as if the Chávez administration has identified some of the major roadblocks to sustained peace but implementation is a far more difficult matter. Chávez wants to be seen as a defender of his populist principles and, therefore, unabashedly takes on the United States and other Latin American countries that do not support his ideals. Instead, he seeks allies like Russia and China that are willing to supply him with the military equipment and weapons that Venezuela used to purchase from the U.S. That will lessen his dependence on the United States and strengthen his 21st Century Socialism. He must, however, be careful not to needlessly engage in a self-destructive overreaction to his distaste for the United States.

Upon the electoral defeat of the constitutional reform proposal in 2007, Chávez realized that he must reassess his policies to increase his support from the rest of the country that voted against his constitutional reform. Ramón Carrizales, Venezuela's Vice-President, said the period following the electoral defeat is part of the "permanent" process of "Revision, Rectification, and Re-advance"--the "three Rs." This process is to self-criticize and correct mistakes they believe they have made previously.

Economically, the government is now pushing to diversify its economic base so there is a lower dependency on oil and other countries to provide food to Venezuela. Recently Chávez stressed that "we should move away from the oil-based production model. The future of the country is in the land, in the agricultural project, not in petroleum. Food production is the most important."[35] This action is in line with rebalancing the three societal dimensions. In addition, according to Carrizales, the government does not want to isolate the private sector and is reengaging with private businesses. The government wants to improve the situation by lifting price controls on certain products and reducing obstacles to imports.

These adjustments are a start to alleviate the disenfranchised portion of the middle class and elite and to achieve his future vision, but there are additional problems in this dimension that may continue to cause instability. One issue is the government's nationalization of estates and industries, making social property for the poor. Chávez said that by turning large, idle estates into Socialist Production Units (UPS), it is now the workers' responsibility to transform production from capitalist to socialist. His vision is to increase agricultural productivity so the Venezuela people can be better able to sustain themselves.

Chávez should continue to help the poor of his country but must not inhibit the growth and capability his country can achieve through leveraging the private sector businesses. He must balance the economic dimension carefully because if his main source of income, petroleum, becomes his only source of income, he increases the risk for disaster from market fluctuations.

To balance the security dimension, Chávez needs to purge his country of narco-trafficking and other crime. He must continue his assistance to Colombia along the border and not supply military or moral assistance to the FARC. He must understand that by aiding the insurgents in any way and increasing the instability in Colombia, it will cause secondary and tertiary effects that may disrupt his government also.

Finally, at the political dimension, it seems as if Chávez does not want this dimension balanced. The perception to many is that he is striving for greater and greater power to achieve a semi-authoritarian position. His actions, such as nationalizing industry and taking lands for the

---

[35]James Suggett, "Chávez Increases Corn Prices, Announces Shift from Oil to Food in Venezuela," *Venezuela News, Views, and Analysis*, Venezuelanalysis.com (27 April 2008), http://www.venezuelanalysis. com/news/3389 (accessed 29 April 2008).

poor, also promote this perception. To balance the political dimension, Chávez must understand the repercussions his actions and policies have on the middle class and the elites. If he does not address this problem, he risks another possible coup attempt. He is also trying to strengthen his newly formed, consolidated political party but there is fracturing among the groups that have agreed to join and other groups that do not want to join. If he does not continue to support the establishment and independence of these and other political parties, the political dimension may collapse. Additionally, he is pushing against the U.S.-sponsored Free Trade Areas of the Americas (FTAA) and advocating a replacement system that excludes the U.S., but in doing so has alienated other Latin American countries in the process like Mexico and Peru. Only four other countries supported his position to abandon the FTAA. It seems as if other Latin American countries and the democratic process currently in Venezuela have helped to keep the political dimension balanced. There is a great danger, however, that Chávez's policies will imperil that balance.

As discussed above, all three AR2 societal dimensions must be balanced in Venezuela in order to have a lasting peace. Although his policies thus far have done well for the poor of his country, Chávez's social programs are not enough to keep his country stabilized in the long term. He is not alone in his quest for stability however. His neighbor, Colombia, is also in the middle of an AR2 process and is facing an imbalance in its AR2 process. However, Colombia's methods for implementing the AR2 process are vastly different.

COLOMBIA

Roots of Conflict: The Need for AR2

Colombia's AR2 process, as with Venezuela's, also involved a long history of conflict. Originally a Spanish settlement, Colombia has maintained a democratic tradition of regular, free elections with political parties and citizen participation since its first representative government in

1810. It is a country dominated by elite groups born from the social hierarchy indicative of Spanish colonization. The upper class, constituting 5 percent of the population, is overwhelmingly white; the middle class, 20 percent, is mostly mestizo; and the lower class, 75 percent, is proportionately mestizo, Afro-Colombian, and indigenous.[36] Most indigenous people and Afro-Colombians live in rural areas--the former in barren and inaccessible regions and the latter in the Caribbean and Pacific coastal regions and tropical valleys.

Two political parties, the Liberals and the Conservatives, have dominated the political landscape in Colombia for over 150 years. The Liberals wanted a decentralized government, state control over education and other civil matters, and broader suffrage. The Conservatives, mainly Bolívar's supporters, wanted a strong centralized government, alliance with the Roman Catholic Church, and a limited franchise. These parties have alternated rule throughout most of those years as the dominant ruling party and typically those leaders have also been the political leaders and business leaders. These political factions separate along economic lines; between the landed and the non-landed. The two most powerful are the landed agricultural groups and the landed merchants. The reason these groups traditionally hold the most power is that economically, Colombia has historically been an agricultural-based economy with coffee as its major crop until oil replaced it as the nation's leading legal export. Colombia, however, is also known for its production of heroin, cannabis, and cocaine, which has brought riches to some but has seriously disrupted the fabric of Columbian society with its violence. Cocaine exports alone accounted for about 25 percent of Columbia's foreign exchange earnings.[37] It would seem as if conflicts would separate among class lines between the poor and the rich but in reality, politics drove the conflicts at the time.

---

[36]Ibid.

[37]Infoplease.com, Encyclopedia Colombia- Economy, http://www.infoplease.com/ce6/world/A0857441.html (accessed 20 February 2008). Colombia: Economic Development and Policy under Changing Conditions (1984)

Both the Liberals and the Conservatives were multi-class parties with the middle-class, urban and rural poor led by elites. The peasants and the urban masses usually aligned themselves with the owners whose land the workers had access. It has often been said that in Colombia, one is born Liberal or Conservative.[38] Loyalties to the separate parties make the Colombia structure unique in that the depth of affiliation has endured since the nineteenth century and during that time, numerous civil wars between the two parties erupted in one part of the country or another. The bitter rivalries between the two parties and the seemingly interminable fighting culminated in the great War of a Thousand Days (1899 to 1902) that affected the whole country killing about 100,000 people.[39] After 40 years of peace, civil wars once again erupted in a period of intense violence from 1946 to 1965 known as La Violencia. In 1958, a political pact known as the National Front (Frente Nacional) stated that the Conservative and Liberal party would alternate the presidency and divide political offices for fifteen years. Since then, several administrations have fought insurgencies that have sought to undermine the current political system.

The insurgencies consist of two main rebel groups, the Revolutionary Armed Forces (FARC) and the National Liberation Army (ELN), who have been fighting against embattled government forces for four decades. The emergence of these guerilla organizations in the mid-1960s flourished in Colombia's remote and underdeveloped rural parts of the country until they became the world leader in the production and trafficking of illegal drugs in the 1970s and 1980s. The Colombian armed forces, expanded mainly to fight the rebel groups, have improved their battlefield performance since suffering embarrassing defeats at the hands of the FARC from 1996 to 1998. With the election of President Álvaro Uribe Vélez in 2002 and the United States' assistance, the Uribe government stepped up actions against the guerillas. Offensives carried out

---

[38]Catherine C. LeGrand, "The Colombian Crisis in Historical Perspective," McGill University, April 2001, http://socrates.berkeley.edu:7001/Events/conferences/Colombia/workingpapers/ working_paper_legrand html (accessed 12 March 2008).

[39]Ibid.

by the Uribe government have generally been successful. Maintaining control over re-conquered territories, however, remains a challenge since investment in civilian governance is scarce. Though their share of direct involvement in killings and disappearances has fallen in recent years to a current level of about 5-7 percent, the armed forces nonetheless continue to face serious allegations of indirect human rights abuse through collaboration with paramilitary groups. Except for a few high profile cases, past abusers continue to enjoy near-complete impunity. Other internal threats include the narco-trafficking syndicates and paramilitary groups but these organizations often overlap because they are both involved in the illegal narcotics trade. With this history of violence and instability, it is not surprising that Colombia's AR2 process is not complete and is arguably ineffective in its current structure.

AR2 in Practice (in Colombia)

The three societal dimensions of AR2 in Colombia are currently not balanced. In order for AR2 to be effective, there must be a balance between these dimensions. Within the socio-cultural context, using the framework of Dr. Mosser's dimensional diagram, This author would depict Colombia as a country dominated mostly by the political dimension as seen in the diagram below (see figure 5).

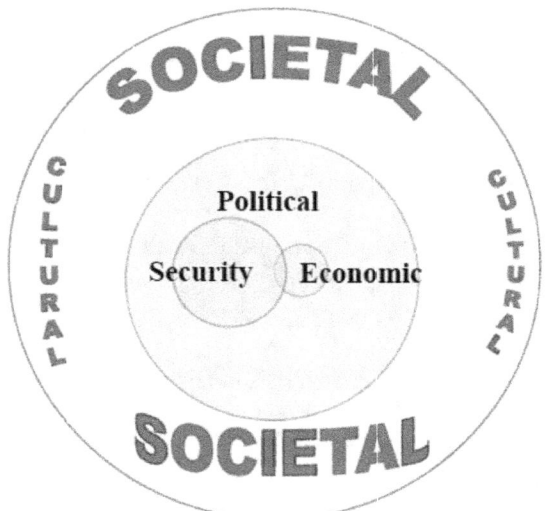

Figure 5.   Colombia's Societal Dimensions of AR2

The best way to look at Colombia and other long-duration conflicts is with a phasing model in which Phase I comprises the short-term fixes or implementations needed immediately to bring the conflict quickly down to a manageable level, or a lower tolerance level, and Phase II comprises the remaining processes to stabilize and balance the system.

Phase I AR2: Incomplete and Imbalanced

In the aftermath of La Violencia, civil warfare gradually dissipated and gave way to the rise of guerilla warfare. The two political parties made a pact alternating the presidency and the government tried to negotiate a peace with the guerilla organizations inside its country. This gave rise to the implementation of military forces within an AR2 framework.

The Colombian army historically has been weak and poor. They lacked any type of prestige or political confidence and were held in unusually low regard by the country's elites. Even as late as 1959, when ex-president General Rojas Pinilla was on trial before the Senate, he felt a necessity to defend the military against charges in the press that all military men were "crude sergeants who barely know how to read and write."[40] However, they are unique in that they have constantly engaged in military operations for almost half a century. Conducting counterinsurgency operations at small unit levels, the army usually operated in small units scattered throughout the countryside patrolling rebel zones. In the post-war system, the military has played a vital role for the two-party political system by disallowing other political parties to enter mainstream politics effectively. The army has been known to take over the local civilian administration unable to perform its duties but because the army approves of its treatment, has

---

[40]Robert H. Dix, *The Politics of Colombia* (New York: Praeger Publishers, 1987), 136.

seldom interfered with the power and politics of the administrations.[41] When military officers have criticized presidential policies, they were removed from position and replaced. An example of this was in 1984 when General Fernando Landazábal Reyes criticized President Belisario Bentacur's policies towards the guerillas, he was replaced. Nonetheless, the political powers give the Colombian armed forces sufficient autonomy financially and organizationally and thus limit militarism and sustain civilian ascendancy in Colombia. Here, the political dimension subsumes the security dimension, as civilian authority has remained consistently predominant over the military.

The civilian governmental structure, with its patron-client networks, has dominated the Colombian landscape. This network is structured around a dependent tie in which the Colombian peasant depended on his patron, usually a landowner, for protection. Spanning generations, this network eventually evolved into a loyal bond used to mobilize the citizenry for political and social purposes. The patron-client network was used extensively to resolve disputes, often violently, between the Liberals and the Conservatives. The two parties are not primarily historical parties of class conflict or ideology and thus have provided a unique stability of the party system. The problem that arises, however, is that as the rural poor have moved into urban areas, with the nature of the Colombian party system, their voices do not seem to be heard. Thus, violence ensues. The nature of the party system tends to exclude the majority of Colombians from having an effective voice in government. When populist movements have emerged in the past, it was done under the auspices of one of the major parties and then eventually reabsorbed by that party.[42] Even the middle class has found it difficult to gain representation in the administration to the extent that they have abstained from voting during several elections.

---

[41]Leslie Bethell, *Latin America: Politics and Society Since 1930* (Cambridge: Cambridge University Press, 1998).

[42]Dix, 116.

During the Post National Front years, there were a series of cease-fires and truces between the Colombian governments and left-wing guerillas, paramilitary self-defense forces, and drug cartels. Either sides, at one time or another, broke those agreements. In 1990, narco-terrorists assassinated three presidential candidates during the election campaign and on the other side, 2,000 to 3,000 of the FARC's demobilized members were murdered.[43] Negotiations with organizations such as the Democratic Alliance/M-19 led to a peace agreement with the reintegration of M19 back into society and political life. The M-19 even participated in the process of enacting a new constitution in 1991 that reformed Colombia's political institutions to include the reestablishment of a Vice President and an appeal system allowing individuals increase of constitutional justice.

These Post National Front years determined a stronger need for AR2 as the activities of guerilla forces grew, paramilitary groups expanded, and drug production increased. Actions within all three societal dimensions of AR2 were used to try to prevent the growing instability within the country. So why did AR2 not work? The answer lies in the imbalance and incompleteness of the three dimensions. Two administrations, the Andrés Pastrana (1998 to 2002) and Alvaro Uribe (2000 to Present) Administrations implemented a strategy called "Plan Colombia" beginning in 1999 to combat narco-terrorism; jump start economic recovery; fortify democratic institutions and respect for human rights; and provide humanitarian assistance to internally displaced persons. In November 1998, President Pastrana tried to set conditions to negotiate with the FARC by giving them roughly 40 percent of the country's land as a neutral territory for peace negotiations.[44] Instead of the FARC reaching an agreement, they continued conducting attacks against the government, fighting with paramilitaries for control of cocoa-producing lands, and kidnapping. His implementation of his policies failed to work. In February

---

[43]US Department of State, Bureau of Western Hemisphere Affairs, "Background Note: Colombia," March 2008, http://www.state.gov/r/pa/ei/bgn/35754.htm (accessed 16 March 2008).

[44]Brown and Smith, 2.

2002, Pastrana broke off talks and ordered the military to retake the rebel-held zone. Later, he also broke off talks with the country's second-largest rebel group, the National Liberation Army (ELN). When President Uribe was elected president, he continued the broad goals of Plan Colombia and a new "Democratic Security" strategy that included a sharp rise in military spending and a dramatic increase of troops and police deployed throughout the national territory. This strategy also included negotiations to demobilize pro-government paramilitary militias. On the surface, Uribe's policies seem to be working. The United States, for example, appropriated billions of dollars to Colombian aid in counter-narcotics and counter-terrorism to help improve Colombia's security posture. In addition, Uribe's negotiations with paramilitary groups have led to the demobilization of over 31,000 members of the right-wing Colombian Self-Defense Forces (AUC) paramilitary group that was originally formed as part of the Colombia military's brutal strategy to undermine leftist guerillas by systematically attacking civilian populations. In May 2006, boosted by an improving economic and security situation, Uribe won a second term.

Economically, over the past few years Colombia has been able to maintain its GDP growth: according to National Administrative department of statistics (DANE), if one compares the second trimester of 2006 to the second trimester of 2007, the GDP went up to 6.87 percent. Unemployment has remained relatively steady through 2007 reaching 12.8 percent. According to the National Planning Department, poverty was reduced from 50 percent in 2005 to 45 percent in 2006 and extreme poverty was reduced from 15 percent to 12 percent over the same period. These factors, added to the reduction of insecurity have generated greater trust in national and foreign investors.[45] Many problems, however, still lie beneath the surface, making AR2 incomplete and imbalanced.

---

[45]The World Book, Colombia, Colombia Country Brief, "Development Progress," November 2007, http://go.worldbank.org/L5B8UII7W0 (accessed 25 March 2008).

Even though there is significant popular support for ridding the country of the paramilitary groups, controversy surrounds the policy of granting almost all paramilitary members near full amnesty. The paramilitaries have killed thousands of innocent civilians over the years and have been heavily involved in the drug trade. The paramilitary leaders accused of the most severe atrocities, such as massacres, rape, and torture, are expected to receive significantly reduced sentences.[46] Many Colombians question the paramilitaries' intentions and suspect they will continue to be involved in violence and drug trafficking, especially since some leadership and organizational structures remain pretty much in tact. In spite of progress made above, poverty and inequality remain a main challenge for the country. While other Latin American and Caribbean countries are fighting inequality, poverty, or violence, Colombia must face all three simultaneously.

Economically, Colombia is imbalanced. Colombia's rate of inequality is one of the highest in Latin America where the top 20 percent retain 60 percent of the national income, in strong contrast to Sweden where the top 20 percent retain 34 percent of the national income. Furthermore, over 80 percent of U.S. aid to Colombia since 2000 has gone to train and equip Colombian security forces while the remaining 20 percent has gone to humanitarian assistance, judicial reform, and rural development.[47] Inequality has therefore been one of Colombia's most longstanding features and is a characteristic that often supports violence. Even when economic growth has managed to reduce poverty, inequality is present.

Colombia has also increased fumigation of coca plantations but development aid for alternative means of economic livelihood has been slower to arrive or has failed to improve people's lives. For example, legal crop substitution is often less profitable with a stagnation in

[46]Connie Veillette, Congressional Research Service, Report, "Plan Colombia: A Progress Report" (Washington, DC: The Library of Congress, 11 January 2006), http://digital.library.unt.edu/govdocs/ crs//data/2006/upl-meta-crs-8270/RL32774_2006Jan11.pdf (accessed 20 December 2007).

[47]HLB International, "Doing Business in Colombia," November 2007, www hlbi.com/dbifiles/ dbi_pdf/DBI%20Colombia%20A4.pdf (accessed 17 May 2008).

crop prices, the high costs of vehicles, and transportation on immature roadways cutting into the profits. There has been a large neglect and undervaluing of all things non-military with policymakers placing a lower priority on governance and development aid. These programs are often mismanaged, corrupt, or ill-funded. Because of this, coca cultivation moves to other parts of the country or is reestablished when fumigation subsides in an area. In the mid- to long-term, coca production is not subsiding. With Colombia exporting 80 to 90 percent of its drug production to the United States and the FARC controlling approximately 70 percent of the Colombian cocaine trade, the demand for the product still remains strong.[48]

Although many paramilitary blocs demobilized, many branches continue their activities with few changes besides the removal of their uniforms. They increasingly resemble Italian-style mafias where they are involved in politics, allowing them to tap into government treasuries. The problem arises when these paramilitaries do not trade their weapons for politics but instead use both.

These problems are disruptive to the society and if applied to Michael Lund's conflict cycle can elevate Colombia from an unstable peace to crisis. How can one stop the escalation?

Phase II AR2: How to Make it Work

To President Uribe's credit, he has made significant progress during his six years in office and AR2 is a long process. Unfortunately, successes are often fragile and reversible, especially under the conditions present in Colombia. There needs to be a downward shift on the conflict cycle towards a stable peace, and this author proposes the key to that is to examine the three societal dimensions of AR2 and focus upon balancing them.

---

[48]Department of Justice, "High-ranking Member of Colombian FARC Narco-Terrorist Organization Convicted on U.S. Drug Charges," 20 February 2007, http://www.justice.gov/opa/pr/2007/February/07_crm_094 html (accessed 18 March 2008).

There is a disparity in the AR2 model as discussed previously and furthermore, with a dramatic expansion of the security dimension because of the implementation of Plan Colombia and the focus upon security (as seen in Figure 6 below), there is a greater danger of "overcorrection" in which the security dimension is expanding so rapidly that the imbalance will remain but with a different structure. Security will then replace the political dimension as the dominant dimension.

As noted earlier in Phase I, President Uribe has implemented short-term fixes to Colombia's problems with a relatively high level of success. Phase II AR2 needs to focus on mid- to long-term solutions in order to break the conflict cycle and remain in the stable peace level. Phase II must overcome the many roadblocks still present at Phase I.

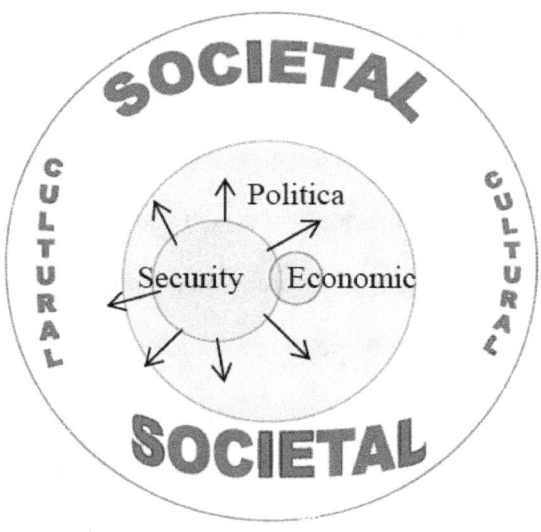

Figure 6.   Possible Shift of Colombia's Dimensions

With the political dimension as large as it is presently and if Uribe's push for security continues at the current growth and expansion rate, there is a danger that the state could assume too much control, making population security its primary function. Having a safe, but imprisoned society in addition to the power of the political sphere can be akin to an authoritarian state. If the security dimension continues to grow at the current pace, it is possible that the security dimension will overwhelm even the political dimension and by gaining more power and means, may result in a future coup or military dictatorship. This will continue the conflict cycle. The economic dimension is small compared to the other two dimensions. The roadblocks here are also substantial and must be addressed to grow this dimension so all three dimensions are eventually balanced.

President Uribe has a plan to take action in each AR2 societal dimension but he must address them so they are put back into balance and maintained in a homeostasis environment. President Uribe is headed in the right direction by addressing all three dimensions. In 2007, U.S. and Colombian officials announced a new six-year "Strategy for Strengthening Democracy and Social Development" to continue the successful Plan Colombia programs, increase access to social services, and support economic development.[49] However, this too has impediments. Under the scope of this plan, he must bring the political dimension in line with the other two dimensions by encouraging new party participation in government, supporting strong local governance, expanding political participation with the poor and middle class, and energizing the peace process with the FARC and ELN. The security dimension must stop expanding at its current levels. Right now that dimension is distorted because of the mistrust of paramilitaries and atrocities committed by both the paramilitaries and Colombian military. There must be internal policing of this dimension. By enacting the Justice and Peace Law and through the Congress' hard stance on

---

[49]The Center for International Policy, "Below the Radar: U.S. Military Programs with Latin America, 1997-2007," March 2007, http://ciponline.org/colombia/cipanal.htm (accessed 29 September 2007).

paramilitary amnesty, this dimension may stabilize through increased human security, justice, and the reintegration of former paramilitaries and gang members.[50] Uribe must move the society to where security gains are institutionalized and where violence is the exception.[51] The economic dimension is the weakest of the three and also needs balancing. President Uribe's new strategy may provide that assistance. This strategy must encompass investment into poor neighborhoods and infrastructure, drug eradication, and free trade expansion. The United States Congressional budget still has 76 percent of its Colombian appropriations going towards Colombia's security apparatus, virtually identical to previous years.[52] If the new plan is to survive and become successful, the same amount of budgeting, if not more, should go to economic programs.

To balance these three dimensions will take time and Colombia is headed in the right direction but it must be watched and tended carefully so the conflict cycle does not continue. Furthermore, the instability in Colombia is not confined to its borders. If instability in Colombia expands, Colombia's neighboring countries will feel the effects of that expansion.

Comparison of AR2 in Venezuela and Colombia

As neighbors in Latin America with a common ancestry, both Venezuela and Colombia have undergone cycles of conflict, whether from events like military coups in Venezuela or a dramatic civil war like La Violencia in Colombia, to emerge as democratic, civilian-led democracies. Both countries have had many successes even though one country follows a more capitalist approach and the other country follows a more socialist approach. Both leaders have

---

[50]2005 Justice and Peace Law is the law governing the demobilization of armed groups in Colombia and provides de facto amnesties to include granting legal and economic benefits for those not under investigation for human rights offenses.

[51]Democratic security trends in Colombia depict a decrease in violent crimes from around 2002 until present. See Economist, "The Uribe Temptation," (19-25 April 2008): 46-47.

[52]The Center for International Policy's Colombia Program, "A Guide to the House Bill's Proposed Changes to Colombia Aid," http://www.cipcol.org/?p=426 (accessed 19 April 2008).

gained substantial power and popularity in their respective countries and have gained semi-authoritarian status. Both countries, that were once fractured, still have instability because of an imbalance of the three societal dimensions of AR2, the political, economic, and security dimensions. Venezuela's society is dominated with the economic dimension that threatens to engulf it if the country does not diversify its source of wealth. Other problems with the other two dimensions include class-based tensions and the increase in violent crimes and kidnappings. Colombia's society, on the other hand, is dominated with the political dimension's political-based conflicts with an expanding security dimension that threatens to consume the society if not properly managed. In addition, negligence of the economic dimension here can broaden the chasm between the elites and the poor and middle class.

As stated in the introduction, Venezuela and Colombia have followed different paths along the AR2 process because of the type of conflicts in their history and the needs of their population after those conflicts. Venezuela follows a strong populist strategy to fight United States imperialism and liberate the poor whereas Colombia follows a strong security strategy facing the extreme violence and insurgency in their country. Although Venezuela and Colombia have differing AR2 constructs, there are linkages between the two that cannot be summarily dismissed. Their AR2 process is not mutually exclusive because Colombia's AR2 process and strategies affect Venezuela and vice versa.

Venezuela has many AR2 ties with Colombia. Their shared boundary is porous and activity across their border affects all three AR2 societal dimensions. In terms of the economic, there is cross-border narco-trafficking that impacts both countries, and Venezuela and Colombia have increased relations in trade and investment. In 2007, Colombia's exports to Venezuela climbed to $4 billion.[53] In the security dimension, guerilla and insurgent activities spread from

---

[53]Simon Romero, "Leaders of Venezuela and Colombia, Ideological Opposites, Are Tightening Ties," *New York Times*, 19 October 2007, http://www.nytimes.com/2007/10/19/world/americas/19latin.html (accessed on 18 March 2008).

Colombia into Venezuela mainly due to drug trafficking but also because it provides a safe haven for the FARC and other rebel groups from the Colombian military forces. Finally, in the political dimension, the poor of Colombia undoubtedly see the progress the socialist system grants the poor of Venezuela, possibly stirring the discontent in Colombia. Unless Colombia addresses this issue, the FARC and ELN retain a portion of the population that supports and aids its struggles. Another political correlation has been the ability for Chávez to help Colombia with hostage negotiations. For example, Uribe welcomed Chávez's offer to broker a hostage negotiation for the release of dozens of captives held by the FARC. The connections of the dimensions between both countries are in actuality an interlocking of six dimensions where each country's three dimensions may affect those of the other's. Like a compound molecular structure, the countries are inextricably bounded to each other as figure 7 demonstrates.

Figure 7.   Integrated AR2 Dimensional Model

This diagram represents an AR2 model that is balanced. Here the nodes or "atoms" are the AR2 societal dimensions with the links or "ionic bonds" that connect each dimension to one another. All together, they create a complex system in which the actions taken on one node in one country will affect the nodes of the other country. For example, before Plan Colombia, the security dimension was weak causing an increase in narco-trafficking inside Colombia, and as a second order effect, caused narco-trafficking to migrate into Venezuela. This spillover effect is indicative of the AR2 process in these countries. Moreover, with porous borders and with Colombia surrounded by five other countries, Venezuela, Brazil, Peru, Ecuador, and Panama, one sees this spillover effect also impacting these other countries. In the incident described earlier with Columbia's killing of FARC's second in command, Venezuela was not the only country involved in that escalation of tension. Colombia crossed Ecuador's border for that operation. The AR2 system can therefore involve multiple countries during its process.

There are problems that remain between the two countries that cause difficulties in cooperation through the AR2 process. One such obstacle is a 54-year maritime boundary dispute in the Gulf of Venezuela and the Caribbean Sea.[54] Nevertheless, perhaps the biggest problems are still the ideological disparity and the lack of trust between the two.

Nevertheless, there is a growing dependency between the two countries, for security and economic means. In order for them to both balance their societal dimensions of AR2, they need to work together in spite of their differing ideologies. In the end, a stable region benefits both countries.

---

[54] Alan Riding, "Two Claims of Territory Roil Waters in Gulf of Venezuela." *The New York Times*, 28 August 1987, http://query nytimes.com/gst/fullpage html?res=9B0DEFDA103CF93BA1575BC0A96 1948260 (accessed 18 May 2008).

Conclusion

Venezuela and Colombia are two previously fractured countries in the midst of repairing their societies. Through an amnesty, reconciliation, and reintegration methodology, they have made great progress to mend the problems in their countries, but the process remains unbalanced. By closely assessing the three societal dimensions of the AR2 process, the political, economic, and security dimensions, it is apparent that without a balancing of these three dimensions, the society will remain unstable and will eventually continue the conflict cycle. Venezuela must not close its country off to foreign investment and neglect the middle class as it serves its populist movement. It must also diversify its economic dimension and not solely depend on petroleum as its source of wealth. Colombia must continue its current security strategy but it must also not neglect its economic dimension and the poor of its country. It must increase the people's trust in authorities by addressing government corruption and human rights offenses, and it must focus on the reintegration of the paramilitary groups back into society. Together, they must cooperate to secure the region from those dimensional aspects along the fault lines of collapse. If they do not, an unintended consequence of a policy they enact may limit, impede, or exacerbate a policy or action in the other's country. It is imperative to not only identify the linkages between the stability of the societal dimensions in their AR2 process but to balance them for success.

Bibliography

Bellos, Alex. "Chávez Rises From Very Peculiar Coup," *The Guardian* (15 April 2002). http://www.guardian.co.uk/world/2002/apr/15/venezuela.alexbellos (accessed 18 May 2008).

Bethell, Leslie. *Latin America: Politics and Society Since 1930.* Cambridge: Cambridge University Press, 1998.

Biblioteca Virtual de Simon Bolívar. "El Libertador." http://www.geocities.com/Athens/ Acropolis/7609/eng/bio.html (accessed 5 January 2008).

Bradley, Theresa, and Guillermo Parra-Bernal. "Venezuela's Unemployment Rate Falls to 8.4 Percent (Update 1)."*Bloomberg.com* (25 January 2007). www.bloomberg.com/apps/ news?pid=20601086&sid=aCwKpgiCRX10&refer=news (accessed 18 February 2008).

Brown, Christopher L., and Alyssa Smith. Latin America in Transition: Lesson 2, *Politics and Democracy.* Southern Center for International Studies, 2007. www.southerncenter.org/ la_jan07_lesson2.pdf (accessed 2 April 2008).

Cancel, Daniel, and Sara Miller Llana. "Hugo Chávez Suffers a Blow to His 'Revolution.'" *Christian Science Monitor*, 4 December 2007. http://www.csmonitor.com/2007/ 1204/p01s01-woam.html (accessed 19 May 2008).

Carlson, Chris. "Venezuela Enters Fifth Consecutive Year of Economic Growth." *Venezuela News, Views, and Analysis*, Venezuelanalysis.com, 20 December 2007. http://www.worldproutassembly.org/archives/2007/12/venezuela_enter.html (accessed 16 March 2008).

The Center for International Policy. "A Guide to the House Bill's Proposed Changes to Colombia Aid." http://www.cipcol.org/?p=426 (accessed 19 April 2008).

The Center for International Policy. "Below the Radar: U.S. Military Programs with Latin America, 1997-2007." March 2007. http://ciponline.org/colombia/cipanal.htm (accessed 29 September 2007).

Demarest, Geoffrey. "Mapping Colombia: The Correlation Between Land Data and Strategy." Monograph, Strategic Studies Institute, U.S. Army War College, Carlisle, PA, 2003.

Department of Justice. "High-ranking Member of Colombian FARC Narco-Terrorist Organization Convicted on U.S. Drug Charges." 20 February 2007. http://www.justice. gov/opa/pr/2007/February/07_crm_094.html (accessed 18 March 2008).

Dix, Robert H. *The Politics of Colombia.* New York: Praeger Publishers, 1987.

Embassy of the Bolivarian Republic of Venezuela in the United States of America. "Venezuela's War on Drug Trafficking." http://www.embavenez-us.org/news.php?nid=4182 (accessed 14 February 2008).

Fernandes, Sujatha. "Political Parties and Social Change in Venezuela." *Venezuela News, Views, and Analysis*, Venezuelanalysis.com (22 March 2007). http://www.venezuelanalysis. com/analysis/2295 (accessed 14 May 2008).

Forero, Juan. "Interview With Venezuela's Attorney General." *Washington Post*, 26 October 2007. http://www.washingtonpost.com/wp-dyn/content/article/2007/10/25/ AR2007102501465.html (accessed 18 May 2008).

Globalsecurity.org. "Venezuela- Military." http://www.globalsecurity.org/military/world/ venezuela/intro.htm (accessed 19 May 2008).

Haggerty, Richard A. ed. *Venezuela: A Country Study*. Washington, DC: Government Printing Office for the Library of Congress, 1990. http://countrystudies.us/venezuela/13.htm (accessed 15 December 2007).

Harrison, Lawrence E. *Latin America: Democracy and the Market are Not Enough*. Farmington Hills, MI: Heldref Publications, 1993. http://www.highbeam.com/doc/1G1-14625629. html (accessed 16 March 2008).

Hellinger, Daniel C. *Venezuela: Tarnished Democracy*. Boulder, CO: Worldview Press, Inc., 1991.

Herman, Donald L. *Democracy in Latin America: Colombia and Venezuela*. New York: Praeger, 1988.

Hidalgo, Manuel. "A Petro-State: Oil, Politics and Democracy in Venezuela." Working Paper 49/007, 11 June 2007. www.realinstitutoelcano.org/documentos/WP2007/WP49-2007_Hidalgo_Petro-State_Venezuela.pdf (accessed 8 March 2008).

HLB International. "Doing Business in Colombia." November 2007. www.hlbi.com/ dbifiles/dbi_pdf/DBI%20Colombia%20A4.pdf (accessed 17 May 2008).

International Institute for Democracy and Electoral Assistance (IDEA). *Reconciliation After Conflict: Policy Summary*. Sweden: Bulls Tryckeri, 2003. www.idea.int/publications/ reconciliation/upload/policy_summary.pdf (accessed 15 March 2008).

Janicke, Kiraz. "Venezuela President's Amnesty for Coup Participants is Praised and Criticised." *Venezuela News, Views, and Analysis*, 3 January 2008. http://www.venezuelanalysis. com/news/3030 (accessed 15 May 2008).

Kline, Harvey F. *Colombia: Portrait of Unity and Diversity*. Boulder, CO: Worldview Press, Inc., 1983.

"Latin America and the United States: Spring Break." The Economist, 3 March 2007. http://www.economist.com/displayStory.cfm?Story_ID=E1_RSRDNNN (accessed 17 May 2008)

LeGrand, Catherine C. "The Colombian Crisis in Historical Perspective." McGill University, April 2001. http://socrates.berkeley.edu:7001/Events/conferences/Colombia/ workingpapers/working_paper_legrand.html (accessed 12 March 2008).

Library of Congress, Federal Research Division. "Country Profile: Venezuela" (March 2005)." http://lcweb2.loc.gov/frd/cs/profiles/Venezuela.pdf (accessed 20 December 2007).

Manwaring, Max G. "Venezuela's Hugo Chávez, Bolivarian Socialism, and Asymmetric Warfare." Research Project, Strategic Studies Institute, U.S. Army War College, Carlisle, PA: October 2005.

Mosser, Michael W. "The 'Armed Reconciler:' The Military Role in Amnesty, Reconciliation, and Reintegration Process." *Military Review* 87, no. 6 (November-December 2007): 13-19.

Parsa, Misagh. *States, Ideologies, & Social Revolutions*. Cambridge, UK: Cambridge University Press, 2000.

Reel, Monte. "Crime Brings Venezuelans Into Streets: Large Protests Over Soaring Homicide Rate Create Political Challenge for Chávez." *Washington Post*, 10 May 2006: A17.

Riding, Alan. "Two Claims of Territory Roil Waters in Gulf of Venezuela." *The New York Times*, 28 August 1987. http://query.nytimes.com/gst/fullpage.html? res=9B0DEFDA103CF93BA1575BC0A961948260 (accessed 18 May 2008).

Rodán, Mary. *Blood and Fire: La Violencia in Antioquia, Colombia, 1946-1953.* North Carolina: Duke University Press, 2002.

Romero, Simon. "Leaders of Venezuela and Colombia, Ideological Opposites, Are Tightening Ties." *New York Times*, 19 October 2007. http://www.nytimes.com/2007/10/19/ world/americas/19latin.html (accessed 18 March 2008).

Ropers, Norbert, Dr. *Peace-Building, Crisis Prevention and Conflict Management: Technical Cooperation in the Context of Crises, Conflicts and Disasters.* Federal Republic of Germany: Deutsche Gesellschaft für, 2002. www.gtz.de/de/dokumente/en-crisis-prevention-and-conflict-management.pdf (accessed 18 February 2008).

State, Society and Governance in Malenesia Project. "Conflict and Post-conflict: Asia Pacific Dimensions" Workshop, University House, Australian national University, 23-24 September 2002. http://rspas.anu.edu.au/papers/melanesia/conference_papers/2002/ 0209_conflict_Report.pdf (accessed 18 February 2008).

Stratfor, Strategic Forecasting, Inc. "Venezuela: Security Takes a Backseat." 2 November 2007. http://www.stratfor.com/analysis/venezuela_security_takes_backseat (accessed 18 February 2008).

Suggett, James. "Chávez Increases Corn Prices, Announces Shift From Oil to Food in Venezuela" *Venezuela News, Views, and Analysis*, Venezuelanalysis.com (27 April 2008). http://www.venezuelanalysis.com/news/3389 (accessed 29 April 2008).

Sullivan, Kevin. "Chávez Tightening Grip on Judges, Critics Charge Venezuelan President's Reforms Called Threat to Rule of Law, Attempt to Undermine Recall Effort". *Washington Post Foreign Service*, 20 June 2004: A24. http://www.washingtonpost.com/ wp-dyn/articles/A54913-2004Jun19.html (accessed 18 March 2008).

US Department of State. Bureau of Western Hemisphere Affairs. "Background Note: Colombia." March 2008. http://www.state.gov/r/pa/ei/bgn/35754.htm (accessed 16 March 2008).

US Department of Justice. Federal Bureau of Investigation. "2007 Preliminary Semiannual Uniform Crime Report- Table 4: Offenses Reported to Law Enforcement, by State by City 100,000 and over in Population." 7 January 2008. http://www.fbi.gov/ucr/ prelim2007/index.html (accessed 19 May 2008).

Uzcátegui, Rafael. "Venezuela 2006: Continued Repression of Popular Protest." *El Libertario*, March 2007. www.nodo50.org/ellibertario/english/repressionof popularprotest.doc (accessed 14 May 2008).

"Venezuela's new bolívar." The Economist Intelligence Unit ViewsWire. 3 January 2008. http://www.economist.com/displaystory.cfm?story_id=10436099 (accessed 19 February 2008).

Veillette, Connie. Congressional Research Service, Report, *Plan Colombia: A Progress Report.* Washington, DC: The Library of Congress, 11 January 2006. http://digital.library.unt.

edu/govdocs/crs//data/2006/upl-meta-crs-8270/RL32774_2006Jan11.pdf (accessed 20 December 2007).

Weisbrot, Mark, Luis Sandoval, and David Rosnick. (CEPR). *Poverty Rates in Venezuela: Getting the Numbers Right.* Washington, DC: Center for Economic and Policy Research, May 2006. www.cepr.net/documents/venezuelan_poverty_rates_ 2006_05.pdf (accessed 9 March 2008).

The World Book. Colombia. Colombia Country Brief. "Development Progress." November 2007. http://go.worldbank.org/L5B8UII7W0 (accessed 25 March 2008).